living
life
dying
death

A Guide to Healthy Conversations
about Death and Dying to Inspire Life and Living

living life
    dying death™

Healthy conversations about death and dying.
www.livinglifedyingdeath.com

Illustrations by Anthony Taylor

Author Photograph by Colleen Holman
www.photographybycolleen.org

Book Designed by Bruce Elbeblawy
www.bthebookmaker.com

ISBN: 978-0-9679887-9-5

Printed By

www.FiveStarPublications.com

The art of living well and the art of dying well are one.

Epicurus

For Matthew

The subject tonight is Love
And for tomorrow night as well,
As a matter of fact
I know of no better topic
For us to discuss
Until we all
Die!

Hafiz ~ Mystic Poet

Acknowledgements

Love and gratitude to my family — Matt, Emily, Adam, Anthony, Ray, Elizabeth and Melissa. Special thanks to so many friends and family that have supported this book concept for many years.

I also wish to thank Jane Innes for her wonderful editorial talent and friendship.

Love Remains — In memory of my mother Ardys and brother Tony — whose lives and deaths transformed me.

courageous conversations

Talking about death and dying to inspire life and living.

Repeatedly, through her tears she said to me, "...but, I've been meaning to say to him..." Her seriously ill, forty-two year old husband had just been brought into the hospice unit where I was the social worker. He had suddenly become unresponsive and now was actively dying. I listened as she shared with me their lifetime of love and loss.

How many times have you felt uncomfortable searching for the right words to say when someone is seriously ill, dying or grieving?

I have experienced and witnessed many beautiful, tragic, profound, heart-wrenching, life-affirming conversations at the end of life. Why wait to have these meaningful conversations? Share your experiences, ideas, stories, beliefs and questions surrounding death, dying, grief and loss. Quickly you'll discover how deeply life and death are entwined. This book is a call to action for you to find the courage, comfort and confidence to have conversations about death and dying, with the overarching hope that you will embrace living well and dying well.

- In times of health — reflect on, explore and express your beliefs on the very nature of life and living, death and dying.

- In times of health challenges — use this book as a guide to initiate difficult conversations when faced with the possible decline and death of yourself, friend or loved one.

- In times of grief — use this book to bring support and hope to the dynamic experience of grieving.

Death, loss and grief are natural and universal experiences. Never diminish the sadness, suffering or pain that are present in living and dying, but be open to the release, beauty, and love that are possible by living life fully and facing the fear of death.

Open this book and start a conversation! Share stories, exchange ideas, listen profoundly, understand and accept others as you both explore personal meanings of life and death. Courageous conversations about life and death allow the strength and beauty of the human spirit to shine.

table of conversations

love

Start and end every
conversation with words of
love and care.

The words of the
conversation may be
forgotten, but
love remains.

acceptance

Talking about death invites

discovery about

one another.

Part of the human condition

is the need to

feel understood.

What would you like me to

understand about you?

action

Be brave and
open the conversation.

In living and in dying, we
cannot truly know what
another individual needs
or wants until we ask them,
"What can I do for you?"

and

Resist the temptation
to always have a single,
definitive answer. Embrace
the questions that have
seemingly contradictory
"ands", such as "Why do I
feel sad and relieved?"

beauty

Find comfort in the
beautiful moments.

Beauty is infinite
and individual.
Tap into memories.

Ask, "Does beauty ever die
or does it pass on to
other loveliness?"

compassion

Soften your perspective and
"see the best" in others.

Appreciate even the
slightest personal quality.
Be gentle with yourself
and others as you navigate
matters of life and death.

control

Keep an open mind.
True respect and
unconditional love allow
for others to make decisions
that you personally would
not make.

Let go of ways you try to
control other people either
directly or unconsciously.

death

Gain insights.
Facing our own mortality
takes grace and courage.

Do you believe that death
is a door from which to
pass through or a wall from
which there is nothing
beyond?

dreams

Start some conversations

with your own

dream experiences.

Both nighttime dreams

and lifetime dreams hold

a rich source of

conversational topics.

What do you dream about?

dying

Explore the full range
of understandings,
questions and fears about
the process of dying.

Death and dying are
different from one another.
Are you afraid of dying?

euphemisms

Confront cultural sayings
such as "I'm dying to tell
you," "to die for,"
and "over my dead body"
as an opportunity to initiate
conversations about death
and dying. What is on your
"bucket list" of things to do
before you die?

expand definitions

Allow your definitions
and experiences of health,
healing and hope to change
and grow. What do you
hope for in life and death?

experiences

Be a storyteller.
People hold lifetimes of
experiences with loss.

What are your experiences
with death, dying,
grief and loss?

fear

Unmask the mysteries.

What are you afraid of?

Is there anything worse

than death?

food

Sustain with love.
Food is a symbol
and gift of love.

It is difficult to remember
that less food is needed
during the dying process.
A person is not dying
because they are not eating,
they are not eating because
they are dying.

forgiveness

Say the words "I'm sorry"
and "I forgive you."

There is no need to wait for
deathbed confessions.

freedom

Champion the freedom to
make personal choices in
living and in dying.
At the end of life, freedom
and dignity allow for the
dying person to say,
"I did it my way."

good-bye

Say good-bye each time
you part as though it were
the last time you might be
with that person. Power
your good-byes with more
than words — a smile, a
touch or loving tears.

gratitude

Thank You.....Thank You…..

Thank You

for all things big and small.

Spoken words of gratitude

have the power to heal.

grief

Be gentle with yourself and others.
Grief is physical, emotional, mental
and spiritual. Grief is not a checklist
to "work through" or an experience
to "get over." Integrate your loss into
your life and continue the bonds you
have with your deceased loved one
in new and lasting ways.
Love and memories remain after
courageous conversations.

honesty

Talk openly, honestly and
with kind regard. The act of
expressing your thoughts
and feelings can bring a
sense of relief.

What have you been
"meaning to say"
to someone you care about?

hope

Foster hope.

Hope lives in the land of

possibility, mystery and

uncertainty. As humans we

can hold both the possibility

of continued life and the

possibility of dying in our

hearts and minds at the

same time. Hope does not

diminish the reality of death.

humor

Humor soothes.

It really takes a sense

of humor when talking

about the human condition!

Laughter radiates

healthy energy.

impermanence

Change is constant.

The cycle of life includes

creativity and destruction.

What can you create?

What can you let go?

joy

Add in the things that bring

you pure joy —

a little each day.

What would your perfect,

joyful last day

on this earth be like?

language

Choose words with positive

power. When you say a

person "gave up" or

"lost the battle" you

diminish the dying process.

Use thoughtful words of

love, gratitude

and remembrance.

legacy

Live your legacy.
Times of sickness and health
are perfect times to move
forward in creating your
legacy. How do you wish to
be remembered?

life

Live life fully.
What might you do today,
so when you are dying you
can say,
"I've had a wonderful life"?

listen

Resist the temptation to fill
each pause with words.

Listen with your heart,
mind and spirit.
What do you hear?

What are
the deeper meanings
behind the words?

living

Savor living.

Living is a verb:

remember back gently…

plan ahead tentatively…

and live fully today.

When do you

feel the most alive?

loss

Consider the losses you
have experienced through
death, divorce,
pet death, financial changes,
relationships dissolving,
national disaster —
just to name a few. Have
you found new meanings
and values in the losses you
have lived through?

memories

Tell and retell stories.
Sharing stories allows for
discovering new possibilities
and insights. The story does
not change — you change.

mystery

Learn to be comfortable

with the mysteries

of life and death.

Where were you before you

were born? Where will you

go when you die?

nature

Celebrate your connection with
the universe. Death, dying,
loss and grief are natural and
universal. Talking about nature
lends itself perfectly to the
cycles of living and dying. The
ocean, wind, stars, animals, rain,
earth, flowers, sun and moon
have much to teach us. Where
are you in the seasons of life?

non-judgment

Reserve judgment.
Tolerance and compassion
are essential qualities in
courageous conversations
about death and dying.
Remember to apply these
qualities to yourself
and others as you navigate
life and death.

pain

Help carry the burden.
Physical pain, emotional
pain and spiritual pain
can seem overwhelming.
When someone you know
is hurting, just ask directly,
"How can I help?"

paradox

Recognize that
life is bittersweet …

simple and complex
joyful and sorrowful
beautiful and vulgar
comic and tragic
strong and fragile.

patience

Be aware that time can
seem to stand still during
the dying process.

Is patience difficult for you?
What might
unfold in the waiting?

peacefulness

Practice peacefulness.

Where, who, when and what

makes you content,

relaxed and peaceful?

pets

Talk about your childhood
and lifetime pets
who have brought you
love and joy. Pets are a
wonderful example of
unconditional love.

philosophy of life

Explore your

philosophy of life.

What brings meaning, value

and purpose to your life?

relationships

Be present.

What would be left unsaid

or undone if you

died unexpectedly?

What do you need to do to

keep your relationship with

yourself, others and your

higher Source healthy?

respect

Never force a conversation
about death and dying.
There are times in
conversations to "agree to
disagree" or to not state
your opinion altogether.

sadness

Enter into the sadness.

Allow it to be present.

Courageous conversations

sometimes start with

admitting and accepting the

feelings of sadness,

anxiety and fear.

Speak openly about the

feelings of sadness.

silence

Breathe and be
present in silence.

Being with someone in
silence takes courage and
often says volumes.

simplicity

Discover what is essential to

you in living and in dying.

While dying, life is distilled

down to the essential.

spirituality

Engage the spirit.
If you believe in the Divine,
how do you name and
relate to your God?

tears

Let tears flow.
Tears are a release.
Humans tear up when we
are sad, happy, confused,
scared, or even angry. Tears
are a sign that you care.
What do your tears convey?

uncertainty

Remember that not
only does fear live in the
unknown, so too do hope
and possibility.
How might you live fully
today in the uncertainty
and ambiguity of life?

love

Start and end every
conversation with words of
love and care.

The words of the
conversation may be
forgotten, but
love remains.